HOW THEY LIVED

A ROMAN CENTURION

STEWART ROSS

Illustrated by
Alan Langford

ROURKE ENTERPRISES, INC.
Vero Beach, Florida 32964

937
ROS

First published in the
United States in 1987 by
Rourke Enterprises, Inc.
PO Box 3328, Vero Beach,
Florida 32964

First Published in 1985 by
Wayland (Publishers) Limited
61 Western Road, Hove
East Sussex BN3 1JD, England

© Copyright 1985 Wayland (Publishers) Limited

Phototypeset by Kalligraphics Ltd, Redhill, Surrey
Printed in Italy by G Canale & C.S.p.A., Turin

Library of Congress Cataloging in Publication Data

Ross, Stewart.
A Roman centurion.

(How they lived)
Bibliography: p.
Includes index.
Summary: Describes the structure of the Roman
Army and the day-to-day life of a soldier, his
training, weapons, discipline, campaigns, and life
in retirement.
1. Rome. Army – Military life – Juvenile literature.
[1. Rome. Army – Military life]   I. Langford, Alan,
iII.   II. Title.   III. Series: How they lived (Vero
Beach, Fla.)
U35.R67   1987   355.1'2'0937   86–20280
ISBN 0–86592–140–7

CONTENTS

AN EXPERIENCED OFFICER

The sun was setting over the bleak countryside. The young guard, tightly grasping his sword, peered out over the moor below him. Had he seen something moving among the shadows, or was it just his imagination? He was frightened, and needed someone to help him.

Just then he heard the centurion approaching along the wall. The man

stopped and listened, holding tight to his sword. Then he spoke to the guard, "All seems quiet, Marcus." The young man smiled. "Yes, sir," he replied, feeling better already. If the centurion said that all was well, then it was. Centurions were the most experienced soldiers in the Roman army.

In about 1500 B.C. Rome was just an ordinary Italian city. Yet by the time of the birth of Christ, it was the center of the most powerful empire the world had ever seen. This empire was to survive for another 400 years.

The Roman empire stretched from Scotland in the northwest to Syria in the southeast; from the Rhine to the Sahara desert. The Romans brought peace and prosperity, law and order to the countries they conquered. They built fine roads and magnificent buildings, but they could have done none of these things without the help of their splendid army.

The Roman empire as its height, in about A.D. 100.

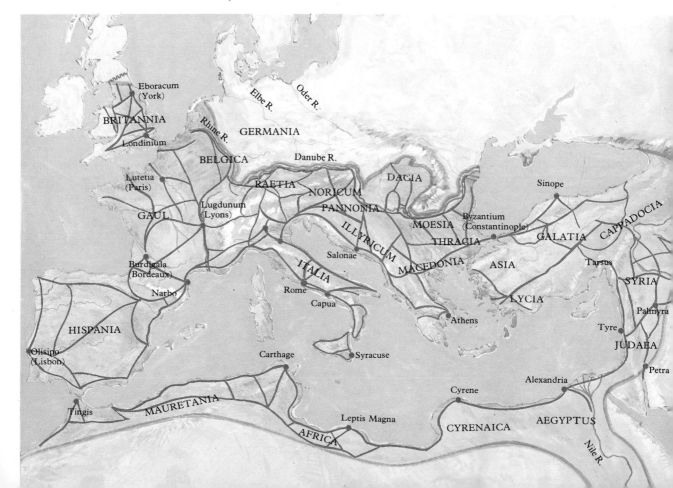

THE ROMAN ARMY

A stone carving of Roman soldiers on the march.

The army built the Roman empire. It was one of the greatest armies of all time. However, it did change as time went by. In the early days of the empire only Romans were allowed to join the army. The soldiers were part-timers. Toward the end of the empire, anyone could join. Even barbarians were recruited to make up the numbers, and fewer and fewer soldiers were Romans. We will examine the army in about A.D. 100, when Rome was at her greatest.

Look at the diagram on the opposite page. The Roman army was made up of twenty-eight legions like this one, with more than 5,000 men in each. These legions were stationed all over the empire. There were three in Britain. Each legion was commanded by a legatus. He was helped by an old professional, called a camp prefect.

A legion was divided into ten

cohorts. The first cohort, of 800 men, was the biggest. The others had about 500 men in each. The emperors had about ten cohorts of special troops, called the imperial bodyguard. Each cohort was further divided into six centuries of about eighty men. The centuries were commanded by the key men of the army – the centurions.

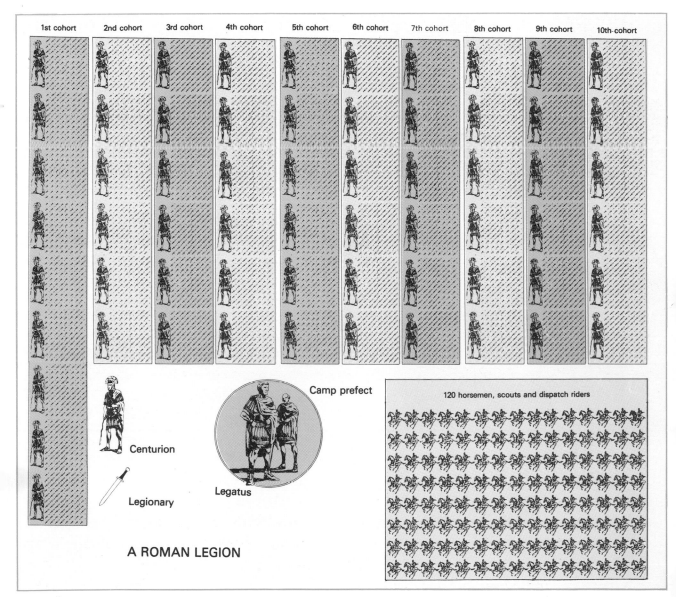

1st cohort 2nd cohort 3rd cohort 4th cohort 5th cohort 6th cohort 7th cohort 8th cohort 9th cohort 10th cohort

Centurion

Legionary

Camp prefect

Legatus

A ROMAN LEGION

120 horsemen, scouts and dispatch riders

THE ARMY'S KEY MEN

Centurions had to be able to read and write and do simple arithmatic.

There were two ways of becoming a centurion. The easy way was to be appointed directly, from outside the army. This happened only to people from wealthy families. Most centurions were ordinary soldiers (or legionaries) who had worked their way up.

There were schools in the army camps where promising recruits were trained. Centurions had to be able to read and write, and do simple arithmatic. Able legionaries were soon appointed orderly sergeants, responsible for the daily password. Then they could become standard bearers, deputy centurions, and finally, if all went well, centurions.

Not all centurions were equal. Those of the first cohort were the most senior. There were four levels of centurion in the first cohort, from rear spear to first spear. The primus pilus (Latin for first spear) was the most powerful centurion in the legion.

The centurions were responsible for the eighty or so men that made up their century. They led them into battle, checked their food, clothes and armor, and punished them if they misbehaved. Centurions carried a vinewood punishment stick. A German centurion called Lucilius was nicknamed "Give me another." That is what he always shouted when he broke his stick on a soldier's back.

All centurions carried a vinewood punishment stick.

CITIZENS OF ROME

All members of the Roman army had one great privilege. They were Roman citizens. Men joined the army from countries as far apart as Britain, Spain or Syria, but once in the army they became just Romans. In the army they were protected by Roman law, wherever they were.

Not everyone could join the army. Slaves, for example, were not allowed to because they were not free. Recruits also had to be over 5ft 6in tall, and in good health. They had to pass a strict interview. Sons of old soldiers were most welcome.

Soldiers had to speak the Roman language – Latin. At first foreign recruits could not understand anything that was said to them, but they soon picked up a few words. Within a year they were fluent Latin speakers. Many words we use come from Latin.

An old soldier presents his son to a centurion for recruitment.

10

Two examples are "miles" (Latin for a soldier), from which we get the word military, and "catapulta," from which we get catapult.

Centurions swore to serve the Roman emperor and obey all orders. They belonged to no country except Rome, and had to go wherever they went sent. Once in the army, many never saw their homes again.

Roman soldiers were often posted to countries far from their homes.

A FRIGHTENING SIGHT

On this page is a picture of the tombstone of Marcus Favonius Facilis. It was found at Colchester, one of the camps of the Roman army in Britain. Marcus is wearing the typical armor of a centurion. Look at the writing below the statue. The letters LEGXX, means that he was a centurion in the twentieth legion.

The tombstone of Marcus Favonius Facilis, a Roman centurion who died in about A.D. 55.

The letters **XX** mean twenty in Roman numerals.

Marcus is wearing the latest kind of armor of the time. It is made of hinged metal plates. Before that centurions wore a cuirass. This was body armor made of little metal scales, like fish skin. Under the armor Marcus wears a long shirt, with leather flaps at the bottom. He wears a scarf to keep his armor from rubbing his neck. Over his shoulder he wears his red centurion's cloak.

Centurions wore leg armor, called greaves. On their feet they had heavy sandals, cut from one piece of leather, with nails in the bottom. These could be very slippery. Marcus has his left hand on his short stabbing sword. He carries his vine-stick in his right hand, while a dagger hangs from his belt on the right.

When going into battle centurions wore bright helmets, with crests running across them. They were a magnificent sight, with their red cloaks, flashing belts and silver-plated armor. No wonder some of their barbarian enemies thought that they were gods.

Barbarian armies often fled in terror from the well-organized Roman soldiers.

LEARNING THE JOB

Training in the Roman army was tough. The centurion was responsible for training the men of his century.

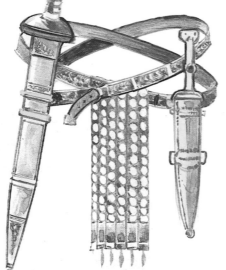

He could remember his hard early days, and would make sure that things were no easier once he was in charge.

Legionaries had to be strong and fit. To achieve this, they went on marches of over fifteen miles. At a quick pace this had to be done in five hours, sometimes carrying as much as forty pounds of equipment. The centurion went along too, to make sure that there were no stragglers.

A legionary's sword and dagger.

A stone carving of legionaries training from Trajan's column in Rome.

The legionaries also ran and wrestled to get fit. But most of the training was in the skills needed to be a soldier. They learned to ride and to swim. Under the centurion's fierce eye they also had to become skilled at stone slinging and camp building.

A large post was set up on the training field. Soldiers had to attack this with wooden shields and swords that were twice as heavy as real ones. When the centurion felt that his men were fully trained, he would give them a mock fight. Real swords and spears were used, but the points were covered. Nevertheless, these battles were dangerous. There was always blood left on the training field when they were finished.

A centurion looks on while his men train for battle.

IN CAMP

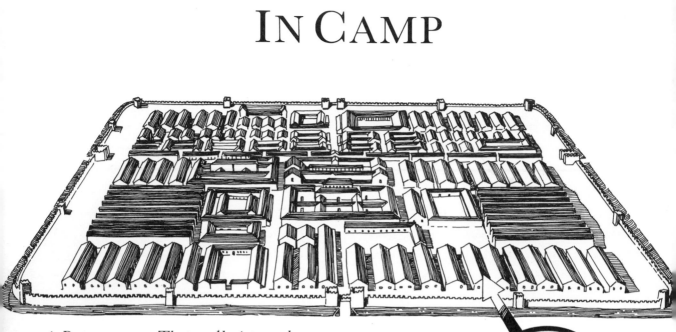

A Roman camp. The small picture shows the inside of a barrack.

Centurions spent most of their army lives in camp. Some of the lucky ones never once fought a battle. The day-to-day frontier work was done by the troops of Rome's allies, called auxiliaries. The legions were kept behind the frontiers, ready for emergencies.

Permanent camps were like villages with strong walls around them. They had everything that the men could need. There were even schools

Camps were often equipped with hospitals. These are Roman medical implements.

16

and hospitals. Each centurion was in charge of a barrack. The legionaries shared small rooms, but the centurion had several rooms all to himself. He also had slaves to work for him.

The centurion's job was to see that the camp ran smoothly. This was a big responsibility. He made sure that the trumpet sounded at dawn – the signal for the men to get up. He arranged guard duty, checked passwords, and organized training and entertainment. If anything went wrong, the centurion was to blame.

A good centurion kept his men very busy, so that they didn't get bored. While some were improving their reading and writing, others would be practicing an attack. The rest might be cleaning their weapons. The centurion and his men had to be prepared to leave camp at any time with only a moment's notice if the alarm was sounded.

The centurion was responsible for the smooth running of the camp.

PERSONAL LIFE

A centurion was usually awakened at dawn by his slave. He had a hot drink and then went to his private washroom. In the winter, his rooms were heated by a special underfloor heating system, called a hypercaust.

A centurion often spent his leisure time eating and drinking with other centurions from the legion.

Before breakfast he was shaved by his slave.

A centurion's breakfast was better than that eaten by the men. He had

porridge, bread and eggs, washed down by a mug of wine. Tea and coffee were unknown to the Romans. He ate lying on a couch, gazing at the pictures that decorated the walls. The largest one was probably a scene from Rome itself.

When off duty, a centurion wore sandals and a comfortable robe (called a toga). For duty he had to wear his uniform. After inspecting his troops, he would spend the morning planning a military exercise. For lunch he would have meat, bread and more wine. Then he would take a short nap.

A centurion's rooms were lit either by oil lamps (top) or by candles placed in candlesticks (bottom).

In the afternoon there was battle training. The evening was spent off duty, having supper with another centurion, chatting, and playing dice. The oil lamp in his room did not give much light, so he went to bed a couple of hours after sunset. Before turning in, he made a final inspection of his barrack to check that all was well.

Dice was a popular game among legionaries and centurions.

19

AT EASE

A centurion's life was not all work. He could go on leave far away from the frontiers, perhaps to Rome itself. Here he enjoyed the life of a great city, for he had plenty of money to spend. If ordinary soldiers wanted leave, they had to pay their centurion a fee.

Even in camp there was some relaxation. Centurions went out for drinks with their friends, or went to the huge public baths. Here they started with a warm bath, then went to a really hot one, like a sauna. Slaves massaged them. They finished off with a plunge in the cold bath.

Large camps had their own amphitheater. This was a huge stadium, like a football stadium, where entertainments took place. Centurions arranged athletic sports between the troops. Sometimes there were chariot races, or even fights. The men loved these rough games. The centurions often had a difficult task keeping them in order.

The Roman baths in Bath, England.

Centurions often had to keep their men in order at chariot races and other sporting events.

The sun-god Mithras has often been called "the soldiers' god."

Like most Romans, centurions were very superstitious and believed in many gods. The most important were Mars, the god of War, and Mithras. The followers of Mithras admired strength and toughness. Many centurions muttered a quick prayer to Mithras as they went into battle.

INTO BATTLE

Every now and again a Roman army had to leave camp and march into battle. This was the moment for which every centurion had been waiting. All his training put to the test.

While the army was on the march, some centurions rode on horses. Other preferred to march with their men – they wanted to keep a close eye on them. Each legionary carried his weapons and armor, a bucket, a pick, a saw, a basket, food, and all sorts of other equipment. The centurion had a difficult job keeping the men moving. He own belongings were usually carried on the backs of horses or mules.

The centurion had to be even more alert when battle started. The Romans attacked by pushing the enemy with their shields, then stabbing them with their swords. The

A stone carving showing Roman cavalry in action.

troops had to be kept close together. When a man was wounded the gap in the ranks had to be filled at once. At the same time the centurion had to keep in touch with other units, and their commanders.

The centurion was expected to lead a difficult attack himself. When the Romans invaded Britain, the centurions had to leap into the sea first and start the attack up the beaches. Defeat for the Romans was very rare. For hundreds of years the centurion and his men were simply the best soliders in the world.

The centurion leads his men through swampy ground on their way to battle.

SIEGE

Not all a centurion's fighting was done in battle. He also had to organize sieges. In A.D. 70 a Roman army besieged Jerusalem for many months. The centurions of four legions took part in the toughest siege of their careers.

The centurions had to make sure that their century was safe from the defenders' missiles. At the same time they had to organize attacks. Catapults and stone-throwers hurled arrows and boulders at the walls. Some of these stones weighted 99 pounds. One knocked a defender's head off—it landed 550 yards away.

Centurions supervised the digging of tunnels under the fortifications. They also ordered the building of enormous towers against the walls.

By climbing ladders inside them, the cenurions led their men straight onto the battlements. Huge battering rams, covered by screens of leather, hammered at the walls below.

Sometimes centurions took their men right up to the city's gates. They were protected from the arrows and stones of the defenders by "tortoises." These were made by soldiers holding shields above their heads, and locking them together, like a roof. After Jerusalem had been finally captured and destroyed most of the centurions took a long, well-deserved leave.

Opposite *Centurions had a vital role to play in a seige.*
Below *A carving of Roman soldiers building a siege tower.*

TRIUMPH AND DISGRACE

A centurion was well paid. He received 5,000 denarii (silver coins) a year. An ordinary soldier was given only 225 denarii. When a new emperor came to the throne, he would often give all soldiers five years extra pay. This was to keep the army friendly toward him.

Centurions were well paid. These are Roman coins of the first century A.D.

There were other rewards for centurions. After a victory, they were given money and wine. The greatest honor for a legion was a take part in a victory procession in Rome. The victorious legions marched through the streets displaying the things they had captured. Crowds cheered and threw flowers. The emperor himself congratulated them. Sometimes an arch was built to commemorate the triumph.

The highest honor for an individual Roman soldier was a crown of grass. Next came an oak-leaf crown, then a crown of gold. This was given to the first man over the wall in a siege. Centurions could also earn a silver spear.

Centurions were not often punished. When they were, therefore, it was very serious. They might be executed, or dismissed from the army for letting down the legion. Sometimes, if a unit had deserted in battle, it was decimated. This meant that one man in ten was executed. The choice was random. The remaining men, particularly the centurions, were in disgrace for the rest of their army careers.

Opposite *Centurions could be given a number of rewards for bravery in battle. Here, a centurion is given the silver spear by his legatus.*

IN RETIREMENT

A centurion would look forward to his retirement when he might marry and raise a family.

Roman soldiers were not allowed to serve in the land of their birth. Britons, for example, were posted to legions in Jerusalem or Bonn, but never to the camp at Lincoln. This was supposed to keep soldiers from becoming too friendly with the local people.

Until the second century A.D. centurions were not allowed to marry. They were supposed to be devoted to the army. Women, it was felt, would get in the way of their duty. When centurions went on leave, therefore, they rarely went home. It was too far, and they did not have a wife and family to visit.

Normally, if a centurion was not killed, he retired at the end of his twenty-five years in the army. He was given generous amounts of land and money. Most settled in the country where they had served. By this time they felt more at home there than in the country of their birth.

A retired centurion might marry and raise a family. Many bought farms or small businesses. They had given a good deal to the empire. In return, they were allowed to spend their final years in well-earned peace and prosperity.

A centurion's retirement villa may have been decorated with beautiful floor mosaics like this one in Littlecote House in Wiltshire, England.

THE END OF THE EMPIRE

From about A.D. 200 onward the Roman empire was in trouble. Fierce tribes attacked over the frontiers. The army became weaker. The Romans never had a good cavalry, and the legionaries found it difficult to deal with the skilled horsemen who now attacked them.

Fewer and fewer Roman citizens joined the army. The Romans squabbled among themselves and in A.D. 286 they divided the empire into two parts. Finally, in A.D. 476, Rome itself was captured by ferocious barbarians, called Goths. With the end of the Roman empire, the well-organized world of the centurion was gone for ever.

The Roman empire collapsed with the fall of Rome in A.D. 476.

GLOSSARY

Barbarians   The description given by the Romans to those people living outside their empire.

Barracks   The buildings where soldiers live.

Battering ram   A large pole with a metal end, used for knocking down walls.

Empire   A group of many countries ruled by a single emperor.

Frontier   The edge of a country or empire.

Gladiator   A man who fights with weapons to entertain people.

Province   A part of the Roman empire that had its own governor.

Rank   A soldier's position in the army.

Recruit   A soldier who had just joined the army.

Superstitious   Believing in luck or magic.

Vanguard   The front section of an army.

INDEX

Picture acknowledgments
The pictures in this book were supplied by the following: The British Tourist Authority 20, 26, 29; The Colchester and Essex Museum/Woodmansterne (Howard Moore) 12; The Grosvenor Museum, Chester 23; The Mansell Collection 6, 14, 21; The Museum of London 18 (all pictures); Ronald Rheridan 25.

900362

DATE DUE			
NO 1 '89			
AP 27 '04			
DE 17 '97			
JA 1 '99			
DEC 0 8 2003			